**TOUGH
QUESTIONS**

**REVISED EDITION**

# WHY BECOME
# A CHRISTIAN?

# The Tough Questions Series

*How Does Anyone Know God Exists?* by Garry Poole

*What Difference Does Jesus Make?* by Judson Poling

*How Reliable Is the Bible?* by Judson Poling

*How Could God Allow Suffering and Evil?* by Garry Poole

*Don't All Religions Lead to God?* by Garry Poole

*Do Science and the Bible Conflict?* by Judson Poling

***Why Become a Christian?* by Garry Poole**

*Tough Questions Leader's Guide* by Garry Poole and Judson Poling

**TOUGH QUESTIONS**

**REVISED EDITION**

WHY

BECOME

A

CHRISTIAN?

# WHY BECOME A CHRISTIAN?

# GARRY POOLE

*foreword by* **Lee Strobel**

**WILLOW CREEK**
RESOURCES

GRAND RAPIDS, MICHIGAN 49530 USA

We want to hear from you. Please send your comments about this book to us in care of zreview@zondervan.com. Thank you.

**ZONDERVAN**™

*Why Become a Christian?*
Copyright © 1998, 2003 by Willow Creek Association

Requests for information should be addressed to:

Zondervan, *Grand Rapids, Michigan 49530*

ISBN: 0-310-24508-7

*Interior design by Nancy Wilson*

*Printed in the United States of America*

06 07 08 09 /❖ CH/ 10 9 8 7 6 5 4 3

# Contents

# Foreword

For most of my life I was an atheist. I thought that the Bible was hopelessly riddled with mythology, that God was a man-made creation born of wishful thinking, and that the deity of Jesus was merely a product of legendary development. My no-nonsense education in journalism and law contributed to my skeptical viewpoint. In fact, just the idea of an all-powerful, all-loving, all-knowing creator of the universe seemed too absurd to even justify the time to investigate whether there could be any evidence backing it up.

However, my agnostic wife's conversion to Christianity, and the subsequent transformation of her character and values, prompted me to launch my own spiritual journey in 1980. Using the skills I developed as the legal affairs editor of *The Chicago Tribune*, I began to check out whether any concrete facts, historical data, or convincing logic supported the Christian faith. Looking back, I wish I had this curriculum to supplement my efforts.

This excellent material can help you in two ways. If you're already a Christ-follower, this series can provide answers to some of the tough questions your seeker friends are asking—or you're asking yourself. If you're not yet following Christ but consider yourself either an open-minded skeptic or a spiritual seeker, this series can also help you in your journey. You can thoroughly and responsibly explore the relevant issues while discussing the topics in community with others. In short, it's a tremendous guide for people who really want to discover the truth about God and this fascinating and challenging Nazarene carpenter named Jesus.

If the previous paragraph describes you in some way, prepare for the adventure of a lifetime. Let the pages that follow take you on a stimulating journey of discovery as you grapple with the most profound—and potentially life-changing—questions in the world.

—Lee Strobel, author of
*The Case for Christ* and *The Case for Faith*

# Getting Started

Welcome to the Tough Questions series! This small group curriculum was produced with the conviction that claims regarding spiritual truth can and should be tested. Religions—sometimes considered exempt from scrutiny—are not free to make sweeping declarations and demands without providing solid reasons why they should be taken seriously. These teachings, including those from the Bible in particular, purport to explain the most significant of life's mysteries, with consequences alleged to be eternal. Such grand claims should be analyzed carefully. If this questioning process exposes faulty assertions, it only makes sense to refuse to place one's trust in these flawed systems of belief. If, on the other hand, an intense investigation leads to the discovery of truth, the search will have been worth it all.

Christianity contends that God welcomes sincere examination and inquiry; in fact, it's a matter of historical record that Jesus encouraged such scrutiny. The Bible is not a secret kept only for the initiated few, but an open book available for study and debate. The central teachings of Christianity are freely offered to all, to the skeptic as well as to the believer.

So here's an open invitation: explore the options, examine the claims, and draw your conclusions. And once you encounter and embrace the truth—look out! Meaningful life-change and growth will be yours to enjoy.

It is possible for any of us to believe error; it is also feasible for us to resist truth. Using this set of discussion guides will help you sort out the true from the supposed, and ultimately offer a reasonable defense of

> You will seek me and find me when you seek me with all your heart.
> —Jeremiah 29:13

the Christian faith. Whether you are a nonbeliever or skeptic, or someone who is already convinced and looking to fortify your faith, these guides will lead you to a fascinating exploration of vital spiritual truths.

## Tough Questions for Small Groups

The Tough Questions series is specifically designed to give spiritual seekers (or non-Christians) a chance to raise questions and investigate the basics of the Christian faith within the safe context of a seeker small group. These groups typically consist of a community of two to twelve seekers and one or two leaders who gather on a regular basis, primarily to discuss spiritual matters. Seeker groups meet at a wide variety of locations, from homes and offices to restaurants and churches to bookstores and park district picnic tables. A trained Christian leader normally organizes the group and facilitates the discussions based on the seekers' spiritual concerns and interests. Usually, at least one apprentice (or coleader) who is also a Christian assists the group leader. The rest of the participants are mostly, if not all, non-Christians. This curriculum is intended to enhance these seeker small group discussions and create a fresh approach to exploring the Christian faith.

Because the primary audience is the not-yet-convinced seeker, these guides are designed to represent the skeptical, along with the Christian, perspective. While the truths of the Christian position are strongly affirmed, it is anticipated that non-Christians will dive into these materials with a group of friends and discover that their questions and doubts are not only well understood and represented here, but also valued. If that goal is accomplished, open and honest discussions about Christianity can follow. The greatest hope behind the formation of this series is that seekers will be challenged in a respectful way to seriously consider and even accept the claims of Christ.

A secondary purpose behind the design of this series is to provide a tool for small groups of Christians to use as they discuss answers to the tough questions seekers are asking. The process of wrestling through these important questions and issues will not only strengthen their own personal faith, but also provide them with insights for entering into informed dialogues about Christianity with their seeking friends.

A hybrid of the two options mentioned above may make more sense for some groups. For example, a small group of Christians may want to open up their discussion to include those who are just beginning to investigate spiritual things. This third approach provides an excellent opportunity for both Christians and seekers to examine the claims of Christianity together. Whatever the configuration of your group, may you benefit greatly as you use these guides to fully engage in lively discussions about issues that matter most.

## Guide Features

### The Introduction

At the beginning of every session is an introduction, usually several paragraphs long. You may want to read this beforehand even though your leader will probably ask the group to read it aloud together at the start of every meeting. These introductions are written from a skeptical point of view, so a full spectrum of perspectives is represented in each session. Hopefully, this information will help you feel represented, understood, and valued.

### Open for Discussion

Most sessions contain ten to fifteen questions your group can discuss. You may find that it is difficult for your group to get through all these questions in one sitting. That is okay; the important thing is to engage in the topic at hand—not to necessarily get through every question. Your group, however, may decide to spend more than one meeting on each session in order to address all of the questions. The Open for Discussion sections are designed to draw out group participation and give everyone the opportunity to process things openly.

Usually, the first question of each session is an "icebreaker." These simple questions are designed to get the conversation going by prompting the group to discuss a nonthreatening issue, usually having to do with the session topic to be covered. Your group may want to make time for additional icebreakers at the beginning of each discussion.

### Heart of the Matter

The section called "Heart of the Matter" represents a slight turn in the group discussion. Generally speaking, the questions in this section speak more to the emotional, rather than just the intellectual, side of the issue. This is an opportunity to get in touch with how you feel about a certain aspect of the topic being discussed and to share those feelings with the rest of the group.

### Charting Your Journey

The purpose of the "Charting Your Journey" section is to challenge you to go beyond a mere intellectual and emotional discussion to personal application. This group experience is, after all, a journey, so each session includes this section devoted to helping you identify and talk about your current position. Your views will most likely fluctuate as you make new discoveries along the way.

### Straight Talk

Every session has at least one section, called "Straight Talk," designed to stimulate further thinking and discussion around relevant supplementary information. The question immediately following Straight Talk usually refers to the material just presented, so it is important that you read and understand this part before you attempt to answer the question.

### Quotes

Scattered throughout every session are various quotes, many of them from skeptical or critical points of view. These are simply intended to spark your thinking about the issue at hand.

### Scripture for Further Study

This section ends each session with a list of suggested Scripture passages that relate to the discussion topic.

### Recommended Resources

This section at the back of each guide lists recommended books that may serve as helpful resources for further study.

## Discussion Guidelines

These guides, which consist mainly of questions to be answered in your group setting, are designed to elicit dialogue rather than short, simple answers. Strictly speaking, these guides are not Bible studies, though they regularly refer to biblical themes and passages. Instead, they are topical discussion guides, meant to get you talking about what you really think and feel. The sessions have a point and attempt to lead to some resolution, but they fall short of providing the last word on any of the questions raised. That is left for you to discover for yourself! You will be invited to bring your experience, perspective, and uncertainties to the discussion, and you will also be encouraged to compare your beliefs with what the Bible teaches in order to determine where you stand as each meeting unfolds.

Your group should have a discussion leader. This facilitator can get needed background material for each session in the *Tough Questions Leader's Guide*. There, your leader will find some brief points of clarification and understanding (along with suggested answers) for many of the questions in each session. The supplemental book *Seeker Small Groups* is also strongly recommended as a helpful resource for leaders to effectively start up small groups and facilitate discussions for spiritual seekers. *The Complete Book of Questions: 1001 Conversation Starters for Any Occasion,* a resource filled with icebreaker questions, may be a useful tool to assist everyone in your group to get to know one another better, and to more easily launch your interactions.

In addition, keep the following list of suggestions in mind as you prepare to participate in your group discussions.

1. The Tough Questions series does not necessarily need to be discussed sequentially. The guides, as well as individual sessions, can be mixed and matched in any order and easily discussed independently of each other, based on everyone's interests and questions.

2. If possible, read over the material before each meeting. Familiarity with the topic will greatly enrich the time you spend in the group discussion.

3. Be willing to join in the group interaction. The leader of the group will not present a lecture but rather will encourage each of you to openly discuss your opinions and disagreements. Plan to share your ideas honestly and forthrightly.

4. Be sensitive to the other members of your group. Listen attentively when they speak and

be affirming whenever you can. This will encourage more hesitant members of the group to participate. Always remember to show respect toward the others even if they don't always agree with your position.

5. Be careful not to dominate the discussion. By all means participate, but allow others to have equal time.

6. Try to stick to the topic being studied. There won't be enough time to handle the peripheral tough questions that come to mind during your meeting.

7. It would be helpful for you to have a good modern translation of the Bible, such as the New International Version, the New Living Translation, or the New American Standard Bible. You might prefer to use a Bible that includes notes especially for seekers, such as *The Journey: The Study Bible for Spiritual Seekers*. Unless noted otherwise, questions in this series are based on the New International Version.

8. Do some extra reading in the Bible and other recommended books as you work through these sessions. To get you started, the "Scripture for Further Study" section lists several Bible references related to each discussion, and the "Recommended Resources" section at the back of each guide offers some ideas of books to read.

## Unspeakable Love

Christianity stands or falls on Christ. Yet he left us with a whole lot of hard sayings. But the central scandal of Christianity is that at a point in history, God came down to live among us in a person, Jesus of Nazareth. And the most baffling moment of Jesus' life was on the cross, where he hung to die like a common criminal. In that place of weakness—where all seemed lost, where the taunts of "Prove yourself, Jesus, and come down from there!" lashed out like the whip that flogged him prior to his crucifixion—somehow God was at his best. There at the cross, he expressed a love greater than words could ever describe. That act of Jesus, presented as the ultimate demonstration of the love and justice of God, begs to be put to "cross" examination.

As you wrestle with these tough questions, be assured that satisfying, reasonable answers are waiting to be found. And you're invited to discover them with others in your small group as you explore and discuss these guides. God bless you on your spiritual journey!

Seek and you will find; knock and the door will be opened to you.

—Matthew 7: 7

# Why Become a Christian?

Bertrand Russell wrote a famous book called *Why I Am Not a Christian*. Even though this guide is not a point-by-point rebuttal to his arguments, these discussions will challenge you to draw the opposite conclusion—and to see why there are very good reasons to do so.

You'll begin by looking at some misconceptions about what it means to be a Christian in the first place. Naturally, if you think you're a believer already, you'll probably consider this material irrelevant. Don't. Reconsider the foundation you assume you stand on. Too much is at stake to take this important matter for granted.

You'll also discuss the reasons why Christianity is "bad news" before it's "good news"; why "self-help spirituality" has limits; why Christianity without Christ is absurd; and why Christianity *with* Christ is the best news anyone could ever hear.

Finally, this guide ends with how you do it—how you cross the line and become a follower of Christ. If you think it's so simple that a child can do it, you're right. But if you think adults don't tremble at the impact of the decision, you're wrong. This is a message that will completely change you—forever.

A well-known preacher once gave a message entitled "When Was God at His Best?" The message was a series of questions. The preacher asked, "When was God at his best? Was it when he created the universe and made the great expansive galaxies: was that when God was at his best? No! Was it when he called Abraham and began his new nation: was that when God was at his best? No! Was it when Moses led the nation of Israel out of bondage and crossed the Red Sea: was that when God was at his best? No!" He went on like that for an hour, recounting event after event from history, touching on all the great acts of God working through all the great saints, but every time he answered, "No! That's not when God was at his best."

He finally got to the death of Jesus. "Was it when the Lord died for your sin and made a way for your forgiveness: was that when God was at his best?"

The congregation held their breath.

"No!"

Not even that? The people were getting irritated. *Come on, tell us!* they thought.

The preacher knew he had them, and with a smile he continued. "Do you want to know when God was at his best? It was when he came to you personally, right where you are, with the message of his love and forgiveness, and offered it freely. That's when God was at his best!"

This discussion guide exposes God at his best. He is reaching out to you. He's inviting you to live life with him through his Son, Jesus Christ. You're at the edge of the most amazing adventure of all—that God would seek you out with a personal invitation and say, "Now is the time; receive my gift! Let me give you the fulfillment you were created to have!"

How will you respond?

# Why Would Anyone Think I'm Not a Christian?

## Mistaken Identity?

Imagine turning on the evening news and hearing the top story: Christianity declared illegal! As you sit there in disbelief, the announcer states that anyone who is a Christian will be arrested and will stand trial. Special police forces are already at work, dragging Christians out of their homes.

You turn off the television, hands shaking. You never identified a particular religion to follow, but you were born into a Christian family. Is that enough to implicate you? You think of when you were growing up: your mother made sure you were baptized and attended Sunday school. You were even (you shudder) confirmed! You've visited churches several times over the last twenty years. You also remember that at work you've commented on your "Christian" heritage. Of course, you also know you're as honest, good, and kind as the next guy.

*Oh no,* you think. *I'm toast!*

You hear a sound outside. You sneak over to the window and close the blinds just as a dark blue police van pulls to a stop in front of your house. What will you do? Should you hide? Run out the back door?

There's a knock on the door. You brace yourself for the inevitable and open the door. Two police officers show their badges. You nod. They ask for your mother.

"My mother?"

"Yes, we have information she is here with you."

"Um, no, she flew back to Florida two weeks ago."

"We'll need to look around," one of the officers says as they walk in.

They quickly search through the house looking for any signs of your mother. After a few tense moments, they head out the door. "That's it."

"But . . ."

They stop. "Yes?"

"Well, I just thought . . . the new law . . ."

"Don't worry. We're only arresting Christians, not their relatives," the other officer answers abruptly.

"So you're not here to question me?"

"Like I said," the officer repeats, "we're only arresting Christians."

In this scene, not being accused of being a Christian would come as a relief. Yet so many of the attributes expressed above are what many think identifies a person as a Christian. If you're born in a Christian family and you're not following some other religion—and are not an atheist—then by default you must be a Christian. Right? Especially if you have some Christian exposure in your background. That goes double if you've attended a Christian church with any kind of regularity. Surely that would qualify you to be arrested for being a Christian.

So what kind of evidence is needed to put a person in jail for being a Christian?

I don't need to be born again. I got it right the first time.

—Dennis Miller, comedian

**1.** Describe an occasion when you (or someone you know) believed you had the necessary ticket to attend a special event but for some reason were denied entry.

**2.** If you were to identify someone as a Christian, what definitive factors or reasons would you look for to support that claim?

> I am a son of a Methodist minister, my wife is the daughter of a Presbyterian minister, and I don't know if I've been born again, but I know I was born into a Christian family, and I believe I've sung at more weddings and more funerals than anybody ever to seek the Presidency.
>
> —Walter Mondale, 1984 presidential debate

**3.** Which of the activities in the following list qualifies someone to be a Christian? Check all that apply and give reasons for your answer(s).

____ being born and raised in a Christian family

____ being baptized as an infant or an adult

____ being confirmed

____ attending church regularly

____ observing Christian holidays

____ reading the Bible occasionally

____ serving in the church

____ donating money to the church

____ being a good and kind person

____ participating in Communion

_____ being a formal member of a church

_____ obeying the Ten Commandments

_____ praying frequently

_____ having some kind of spiritual or
emotional experience

**4.** What role do you think religious activity plays
in being a true Christian?

## STRAIGHT TALK

### *Encountering Christ*

As soon as we start pointing to things people do as proof that they're true Christians, we confuse what it takes to *live* as a Christian with what it takes to *become* a Christian. A man and a woman could walk arm in arm, kiss each other, even go to the same home at the end of the day — but that doesn't make them married. For that to be true, a moment must come when they go beyond dating and proclaim unreservedly, "I do." Likewise, people can be associated with spirituality and live out various Christian behaviors without encountering Christ in a significant and authentic way. It happens to people in cults all the time. So the definitive factor in being a Christian cannot be lifestyle oriented — it has to relate in some way to receiving Christ.

Having said that, one would expect someone who *has* encountered Christ to live an obedient Christian life. But an obedient life doesn't save the person — it is simply evidence that Jesus is present and is making his presence known through the person's life.

**5.** Do you think it is possible to have a false sense of security about being a Christian? If you answered yes, name some examples of false hopes. If no, why do you think a person can't be wrong about his or her claim to be a Christian?

## STRAIGHT TALK

### Rude Awakening

The Bible warns of a kind of rude awakening that awaits those who are counting on religious activities to get them into heaven.

> [Jesus said,] "Not everyone who says to me, 'Lord, Lord,' will enter the kingdom of heaven. . . . Many will say to me on that day, 'Lord, Lord, did we not prophesy in your name, and in your name drive out demons and perform many miracles?' Then I will tell them plainly, 'I never knew you.'"
>
> —Matthew 7:21–23

**6.** The people referenced in the above verses were definitely busy doing religious things. What do you think is the difference between an actively religious person who enters the kingdom of heaven and an actively religious person who does not?

**7.** What is the correlation between initially *becoming* a Christian and *living out* one's life as a Christian?

**8.** Do you think a person, to be a true Christian, must be born into the Christian religion, or could he or she be converted into it, or both? Explain your answer.

## STRAIGHT TALK

### *You Must Be Born Again*

The Bible records a fascinating encounter Jesus had with a religious man named Nicodemus. In the middle of their discourse Jesus replies, "I tell you the truth, no one can see the kingdom of God unless he is born again" (John 3:3). This man was not an atheist; in fact, he was well versed in the Bible and a respected teacher. Jesus was certainly not telling an irreligious person to start going back to church. Nor was he telling a hypocrite to stop his sinful actions. He was speaking to a devout member of a local synagogue—a leader, no less—informing him that something was missing in his life. Jesus revealed that this man would not be in God's kingdom unless he became born again.

**9.** What do you think it means to be born again?

**10.** What's the difference between being religious and being born again? Why would Jesus tell someone like Nicodemus, who was already very religious, to be born again?

## HEART OF THE MATTER

**11.** In what ways are you similar to Nicodemus? How are you different?

Enter through the narrow gate. For wide is the gate and broad is the road that leads to destruction, and many enter through it. But small is the gate and narrow the road that leads to life, and only a few find it.

—Jesus (Matthew 7:13–14)

**12.** If you were to encounter Jesus today, would he tell you there's still something missing in your life? Why or why not?

**13.** Why does talking about being born again often create negative images and angry reactions?

## CHARTING YOUR JOURNEY

With this session you're beginning a journey. Keep in mind that you do not need to feel pressured to "say the right thing" at any point during these discussions. You're taking the time to do this work because you're looking for answers and because you're willing to be honest about your doubts and uncertainties. Others in your group would also benefit from hearing about what you'll be learning. So use these sessions profitably—ask the tough questions, think "outside the box," and learn from what others in your group have to say. But stay authentic about where you are in your journey.

To help you identify your progress more clearly, throughout this guide you will have opportunities to indicate where you are in your spiritual journey. As you gain more spiritual insights, you may find yourself reconsidering your opinions from session to session. The important thing is for you to be completely truthful about what you believe—or don't believe—right now.

**14.** Check the statement(s) below that best describes your position at this point. Share your selection with the rest of the group and give reasons for your response.

_____ I still don't understand what it means to be a Christian.

_____ I don't understand the difference between being a good person and being a Christian.

_____ I understand how to become a Christian, but I don't think I am ready to take that step yet.

_____ I'd like to learn more about what it really means to be a Christian.

_____ I am glad to finally understand what being a Christian means.

_____ If believing in Jesus is all it takes to be a Christian, it seems pointless to try to be a good person.

_____ I now have a better understanding of how the Bible would say some people are Christians and others aren't, but I don't agree.

_____ I wish someone would just tell me what hoops to jump through and I'd do it.

_____ I am now sure that I am not a Christian.

_____ I am still unclear about Christianity and whether I am a Christian or not.

_____ I am sure that I am a Christian.

_____ Write your own brief phrase here: _____

_____

_____

## Scripture for Further Study

- Isaiah 55:6–7
- Matthew 7:15–27
- Matthew 22:1–14
- Mark 1:15
- Mark 4:1–9
- Mark 8:34–38
- John 3; 15
- Acts 17:11–12

- Romans 5:12–21
- Galatians 2:15–21
- Galatians 3:6–9
- Ephesians 2:8–10
- Colossians 2:6–7
- Hebrews 3:7–15
- Hebrews 11

# What's the Big Deal About Sin?

## Bad Marketing?

There's a guy on the corner of Third and Meridian holding a fat pack of pamphlets with an outdated drawing on the front. The colors are faded. You know these details because discarded pamphlets litter the street for three blocks in every direction.

He wears a suit and hands out pamphlets to anyone who passes by, all the while shouting at them, "Do you know where you're going when you die, you sinner? You're headed straight for hell, that's where. *Repent* or *burn!*"

The crosswalk light changes, and you realize you will have to walk completely around the block to avoid this nuisance. So you sigh and head straight for him. Better to take the pamphlet and let him scream in your face than to take the long route.

People are veering to the right and left to avoid him, holding up their hands to communicate, "No, I don't want one."

His hand is outstretched, his preacher voice blaring in your ear like a loud horn. There's the familiar-looking pamphlet. You grab it. Just as your fingers make contact with the flimsy paper, you glance up and the guy stares into your eyes. "You sin because you're a sinner!" he exclaims.

Without thinking, you blurt out, "Yes, but I'm a *mild* sinner!"

The man pauses, cocks his head to the left, and smiles. "Well, even *mild* sinners are going straight to hell!" Then he turns to pass out another handful to the next wave of pedestrians.

You stare at the pamphlet with the simple title "Hell: Your Final Destination?" Then, shaking your head, you toss it into the nearest trash can, where it lands on top of a dozen or so previously discarded pamphlets.

Later that day the words linger in your head. Hell. Sin. Repent. Burn.

What's with the negative spin that guy was putting on Christianity? It's confusing. It's depressing. Is that what Christianity is all about: how much we mess up and how bad we are?

Everybody sins. Why would someone spend his entire lunch hour handing out pamphlets and scaring people half to death by screaming in their ears about how bad they are?

That night, walking home, you spot one of those pamphlets out of the corner of your eye. You picture this one fluttering to the ground just a few hours ago after someone missed the trash can. You walk over, pick it up slowly, and toss it in. It never hurts to do a nice thing now and then, does it?

Sin lies only in hurting other people unnecessarily. All other "sins" are invented nonsense. (Hurting yourself is not sinful—just stupid.)

—Robert A. Heinlein

## OPEN FOR DISCUSSION

**1.** Do you think Christianity dwells too much on the negative, because of its apparent emphasis on sin, hell, and judgment? Explain your answer.

**2.** According to your understanding of the Bible, what separates people from God: a propensity to sin, a lack of knowledge about God, or both? Explain your answer.

**3.** Do you believe that people are, for the most part, basically good, basically bad, or somewhere in between? Explain.

**4.** How would you define sin? What are the repercussions of sin, if any?

People have suffered and become insane for centuries by the thought of eternal punishment after death. Wouldn't it be better to depend on blind matter ... than on a god who puts out traps for people, invites them to sin, and allows them to sin and commit crimes he could prevent? Only to finally get the barbarian pleasure to punish them in an excessive way, of no use for himself, without them changing their ways and without their example preventing others from committing crimes.

—Baron d'Holbach, *Systeme de la Nature*, 1770

## STRAIGHT TALK

### *The Sin Problem*

Several verses in the Bible point to the severity of the sin problem.

All have sinned and fall short of the glory of God.
— Romans 3:23

The wages of sin is death, but the gift of God is eternal life in Christ Jesus our Lord.
— Romans 6:23

As for you, you were dead in your transgressions and sins, in which you used to live when you followed the ways of this world.

—Ephesians 2:1–2

Your iniquities have separated you from your God; your sins have hidden his face from you, so that he will not hear.

—Isaiah 59:2

**5.** How do you respond to the biblical claim above that the sin in your life is so offensive to God that it has spiritually separated you from him?

You, Lord, alone are holy, merciful, and full of compassion. Therefore go and smite thy enemies, kill them that hath not faith in thee, and let them suffer terrible torments in Hell, in Jesus' name we ask it. Amen!

—mock prayer, Undernet's Atheism Channel

**6.** The Bible also teaches that the penalty of sin is spiritual death. What do you suppose it means to be spiritually dead?

**7.** Do you think it is possible to be indifferent or neutral toward God without necessarily being antagonistic or hostile toward him? Why or why not?

**8.** The Bible teaches that our sin causes us to become God's enemies (Romans 5:10) and that we are then alienated from him (Colossians 1:21). How might people who appear to be indifferent or neutral toward God really be his enemies?

> You see, at just the right time, when we were still powerless, Christ died for the ungodly. Very rarely will anyone die for a righteous man, though for a good man someone might possibly dare to die. But God demonstrates his own love for us in this: While we were still sinners, Christ died for us.
>
> —Romans 5:6–8

**9.** In what sense is God the one seeking us first, before we seek him?

## STRAIGHT TALK

### A Swim Contest

Imagine that everyone in the world lined up along the coast of California for a contest to see who could swim all the way to the Hawaiian Islands. At the sound of the gun, everyone jumped into the ocean. Some really great swimmers would go quite far, others would get tired after only a short distance, and still others would barely make it off the shore. But one thing is for sure: the end result would be the same for everyone — not one person would be able to swim the entire distance to Hawaii. Everyone would drown.

No amount of preparation or practice would make much difference in the final outcome. Swimming lessons from an expert instructor or the Swimmer's Ten Commandments would be of little value. Only a rescue operation could provide the assistance necessary to cover such a great distance. In a similar way, the distance between God and every one of us — due to sin — is very great. Some of us may appear to be better off than others, but the reality of the situation is that we all have missed the mark and no one has measured up to God's standard. No matter where we are on the goodness scale compared with others, we all need a rescuer.

**10.** How does the above illustration demonstrate that when it comes to our shortcomings before God, comparing ourselves with others seems foolish?

**11.** Some say God rates people using a scale. He places all the good things you've done on one side of that scale, and the bad stuff on the other. Whichever side outweighs the other determines whether you are a good person or a bad person. Do you agree with this analogy? Why or why not? Evaluate the pros and cons of this rating system.

**12.** Does it feel negative or scary to admit that you may have a sin problem? Why or why not?

> Jesus Christ did not come into this world to make bad people good; he came into this world to make dead people live.
>
> —Lee Strobel

**13.** Do you have a tendency to minimize or maximize your sin by comparing yourself with others? Explain.

**14.** How have you or will you deal with the sin problem that the Bible claims all of us have?

## CHARTING YOUR JOURNEY

**15.** Check the statement(s) below that best describes your position at this point. Share your selection with the rest of the group and give reasons for your response.

_____ I agree that the Bible warns about a sin problem, but I don't feel it is an issue with me.

_____ Sin is not something I want to spend my time thinking about. It is all just too negative.

_____ I think there is a difference between "sinning" and just "messing up." Sin is the big stuff. Everyone messes up.

_____ My opinion about sin and its effect on my life has changed.

_____ I think there are degrees of sin with degrees of consequences.

_____ I know that sin is something I can't overcome alone, and I would like to ask for God's help.

_____ I realize that I am a sinner, but I am unsure what I should do about it.

_____ I am overwhelmed with this lesson. How can anyone hope to ever make it if everything we do wrong separates us from God?

_____ I have a hard time believing that God views my little white lie and the terrorist attacks on September 11, 2001, the same way. It just doesn't make sense.

_____ I know that sin is a problem not only in my life but in the world also.

_____ Write your own brief phrase here: _____

_____

_____

## Scripture for Further Study

- Genesis 3
- Genesis 6–8
- Exodus 20
- Deuteronomy 9:7
- Deuteronomy 28
- John 4

- John 8:2–11
- Romans 3:21–25
- Romans 5:12–21
- 2 Corinthians 5:21
- James 4:17
- 1 John 1:8–10

# Why Can't I Make It on My Own?

## *No Handouts*

The local Kiwanis Club was sponsoring a Thanksgiving charity program. Everyone in the group was excited about the opportunity to support the less fortunate. Jeff and Scott teamed up to go shopping for all the ingredients needed for a traditional Thanksgiving turkey dinner complete with all the trimmings. The two weren't gourmet cooks by any means but were quite proud of themselves once they put it all together.

That evening Jeff and Scott drove downtown to the address they'd been given. They talked about how great it would be to see the looks on the faces of this needy family when they brought in the free feast.

Jeff turned his car up and down side streets, gazing intently for address numbers on the front of the small, modest homes. Finally Scott spotted 1121-B and they pulled in the driveway. The car fell silent as the two took in the scene. The house was noticeably in need of repair. The roof was caving in, some of the windows were broken, the paint was practically all peeled off, and the screen door was barely attached by one hinge.

"Uh, hey, buddy," Scott said as he locked his door, "I think I'll wait here. No need for us to overwhelm the people."

Jeff gathered up the feast and slowly approached the house. The wooden porch looked as if it would collapse under his weight. He knocked on the door and a rugged-looking man answered. A toddler came running up. She grabbed the man's hand, swinging back and forth shyly.

Jeff began a clumsy introduction. "I'm from the Kiwanis Club here in town and—"

"Well, what do you want?" the man interrupted.

"Yes . . . well . . . I'm here to deliver these two bags filled with food for you and your family, so you can enjoy a nice Thanksgiving dinner!" Jeff nodded to the toddler, who smiled back and then broke away from her dad's hand and ran off. The man stayed in the doorway with a stern look on his face.

"We don't need your charity. You take your food someplace else."

"But I have it right here. It's all for you," Jeff said quickly as he held out the bags. "It's a gift."

"Don't bother; we don't take handouts." The man started to yell. "We work for our meals. Now you just get on back to your nice warm car and leave us be!"

Why wouldn't these people accept a free gift offered with no strings attached? You can imagine how Jeff and Scott felt. Frustrated. Disappointed. Rejected. Why did the man behind the screen door have to get so upset? How very strange of him to turn away a gift offered in kindness.

If we're going to be damned, let's be damned for who we really are.

—Captain Jean-Luc Picard,
*Star Trek: The Next Generation*

## OPEN FOR DISCUSSION

**1.** Describe a situation in which you or someone you know stubbornly refused to accept the help of another person. What is it about human nature that causes us to refuse assistance?

**2.** Suppose you spent several thousand dollars to purchase a car for a close friend who was in desperate need of one. How would you react if, after you offered your gift with no strings attached, your friend refused the "gift" and instead insisted on paying you fifty dollars for it?

Doubt everything. Find your own light.

—last words of Gautama Buddha

## STRAIGHT TALK

### *God's Solution*

Below is a small sampling of the many Bible verses that describe the solution God has provided for the sin problem we all face.

> In [Jesus] we have redemption through his blood, the forgiveness of sins, in accordance with the riches of God's grace that he lavished on us with all wisdom and understanding.
>
> —Ephesians 1:7–8

> You know that it was not with perishable things such as silver or gold that you were redeemed from the empty way of life handed down to you from your forefathers, but with the precious blood of Christ, a lamb without blemish or defect.
>
> —1 Peter 1:18–19

> God so loved the world that he gave his one and only Son, that whosoever believes in him shall not perish but have eternal life. . . . Whoever believes in him is not condemned, but whoever does not believe stands condemned already because he has not believed in the name of God's one and only Son.
>
> —John 3:16, 18

**3.** According to the previous verses, what is God's provision for solving the sin problem of the human race?

**4.** How does the statement "People are more likely to ignore 'doctor's orders' when they are unwilling to admit they are really sick" relate to our attitude toward solving the sin problem God's way?

God is just, holy and morally perfect. We all stand guilty before God because we fall far short of his perfection. But the Bible also reveals that God is loving and merciful. He has provided a way to escape the condemnation we deserve. He has sent his Son to die for us.

—Cliffe Knechtle

**5.** What are the various ways in which people insist on earning forgiveness or attempt to fix the sin problem by their own efforts?

**6.** Why do you think people strive to solve the sin problem in their own way instead of doing it God's way?

## *Earning Forgiveness*

Several verses from the Bible address the issue of attempting, on our own, to earn forgiveness from God.

> He saved us, not because of righteous things we had done, but because of his mercy. He saved us through the washing of rebirth and renewal by the Holy Spirit, whom he poured out on us generously through Jesus Christ our Savior, so that, having been justified by his grace, we might become heirs having the hope of eternal life.
>
> — Titus 3:5–7

> It is by grace you have been saved, through faith — and this not from yourselves, it is the gift of God — not by works, so that no one can boast. For we are God's workmanship, created in Christ Jesus to do good works, which God prepared in advance for us to do.
>
> — Ephesians 2:8–10

> They asked him, "What must we do to do the works God requires?" Jesus answered, "The work of God is this: to believe in the one he has sent."
>
> — John 6:28–29

> When a man works, his wages are not credited to him as a gift, but as an obligation. However, to the man who does not work but trusts God who justifies the wicked, his faith is credited as righteousness.
>
> — Romans 4:4–5

**7.** What's the difference between a gift and a wage? According to the Bible, is salvation from the penalty of sin a wage or a gift? Give a reason for your answer.

**8.** What is your reaction to the Christian teaching that says it is absolutely impossible to do anything whatsoever to save yourself from the penalty of sin?

## STRAIGHT TALK

### *Our Spiritual Disease*

When a person is diagnosed with an illness, taking certain medications may help ease the problem of the symptoms but do nothing to cure the disease. Other treatments may cure the disease itself and, as a result, the symptoms eventually disappear as well. The Bible teaches that the wrongs we commit on a daily basis are really signs or symptoms of a much deeper problem or disease of the human heart: sin. Performing good works or being a good person is just a temporary treatment of the symptoms of our spiritual disease. Jesus Christ provides the only complete and final cure by forgiving us of our sin and transforming our hearts.

## HEART OF THE MATTER

**9.** How difficult is it for you to admit that you cannot, on your own, bridge the gap between you and God caused by your sin?

**10.** Looking back on your life, what obstacles may have made it difficult for you to trust God? Is trusting God for your destiny easy or difficult for you now? Why?

**11.** In what ways might you expect a person to respond after receiving God's free offer of total and complete forgiveness? How would (or did) you react?

> Whatever was to my profit I now consider loss for the sake of Christ. What is more, I consider everything a loss compared to the surpassing greatness of knowing Christ Jesus my Lord, for whose sake I have lost all things. I consider them rubbish, that I may gain Christ.
>
> —the apostle Paul
> (Philippians 3:7–8)

## CHARTING YOUR JOURNEY

**12.** Check the statement(s) below that best describes your position at this point. Share your selection with the rest of the group and give reasons for your response.

_____ I know I am a sinner, but I'm convinced God will look the other way when it comes to my sin.

_____ I have a difficult time believing that all I have to do is accept God's forgiveness.

_____ I know that sin is a problem, and I know that God and Jesus are the only answers, but I am unsure what that means for me personally.

_____ I am grateful that God has provided a way for me to be reconciled to him.

_____ I know there is no way for me to make it to God on my own, and I am willing to turn over control of my life to God right now.

_____ I'm still unclear as to what part I play in the whole scheme of things. If God wants to forgive me, he'll forgive me, right?

_____ I know that when push comes to shove, all my bad deeds will be outweighed by my good deeds. So I'm not worried.

_____ I know I cannot make it on my own, and this realization has caused a major change in my life.

_____ Write your own brief phrase here: _____

_____

_____

## Scripture for Further Study

- Hosea 4:17
- Proverbs 29:1
- Jeremiah 5
- Daniel 9:9–11
- Matthew 9:9–13
- Luke 15:11–32
- Luke 19:1–10
- Luke 24:13–27
- John 5:39–47
- Acts 4:12
- Acts 12:1–17
- Colossians 1:20
- Hebrews 9:22

# Why Is Jesus So Important?

## Who Wants a Middleman?

Would God ever stop a person from coming to him? If a person really wanted to know God, really prayed hard and loved God, surely God wouldn't keep that soul away from him, would he? Shouldn't we have access to a direct line to God without needing a middleman of any kind?

But then we're told that Jesus is the only way to get to God. This sounds an awful lot like a corporation bogged down in bureaucracy. In such a company it's impossible to go straight to the top guy without running an obstacle course of intercessors and mediators—people who slow down the process and keep us from speaking directly to the person in charge. Instead of talking face-to-face, we're asked to write out our thoughts. Our letter gets sorted and sent to a secretary, then to an assistant, then to a director, then perhaps to the vice president's secretary, and maybe even to the vice president. Then maybe, just maybe, it will go to the president's secretary, who leafs through his mail, deems our message unworthy of the president's time or energy, and tosses it aside.

It's impractical. It's a waste of time. It's discouraging. Why does God need an intercessor or mediator?

> Of all the systems of religion that ever were invented, there is no more derogatory to the Almighty, more unedifiying to man, more repugnant to reason, and more contradictory to itself than this thing called Christianity.
>
> —Thomas Paine, *The Age of Reason*

# OPEN FOR DISCUSSION

**1.** Describe a time when you needed to get through to someone in charge, only to be put on hold, transferred, or even disconnected. How did this make you feel?

**2.** Do you think it is possible to go directly to God without first having to go through Jesus as a mediator? Explain.

## STRAIGHT TALK

### Jesus Has Spoken

Although some people are openly hostile to Jesus, most who do not follow him at least agree he was an amazing leader. At this level, critics and believers alike find in Jesus someone unique in history.

> When Jesus had finished saying these things, the crowds were amazed at his teaching, because he taught as one who had authority, and not as their teachers of the law.
>
> — Matthew 7:28–29

> In the past God spoke to our forefathers through the prophets at many times and in various ways, but in these last days he has spoken to us by his Son, whom he appointed heir of all things, and through whom he made the universe. The Son is the radiance of God's glory and the exact representa-

tion of his being, sustaining all things by his powerful word. After he had provided purification for sins, he sat down at the right hand of the Majesty in heaven.

—Hebrews 1:1–3

**3.** What are some of the benefits the world has gained as a result of Jesus Christ's life and teaching ministry?

**4.** What do you think was Jesus Christ's ultimate reason for coming to this world?

In fact, if Christ himself stood in my way, I, like Nietzsche, would not hesitate to squish him like a worm.

—Che Guevara,
Cuban revolutionary

## STRAIGHT TALK

### *Born to Die*

There is no doubt that Jesus was on a mission when he lived among us — a mission only he could fulfill. His whole purpose in coming to our planet was to give his life so we might live. More than his teaching, more than his example, he was God's rescue operation on earth. Read the following verses to see just how intentional Jesus was about his mission.

The Son of Man came to seek and to save what was lost.

—Luke 19:10

Jesus took the Twelve aside and told them, "We are going up to Jerusalem, and everything that is written by the prophets about the Son of Man will be fulfilled. He will be handed over to the Gentiles. They will mock him, insult him, spit on him, flog him and kill him. On the third day he will rise again."

— Luke 18:31–33

What I received I passed on to you as of first importance: that Christ died for our sins according to the Scriptures, that he was buried, that he was raised on the third day according to the Scriptures.

— 1 Corinthians 15:3–4

Christ died for sins once for all, the righteous for the unrighteous, to bring you to God. He was put to death in the body but made alive by the Spirit.

— 1 Peter 3:18

---

**5.** Jesus' death was more than a tragedy; it was intentional. What was the purpose of Jesus' death? How exactly was that purpose fulfilled by his death on the cross?

> I would never want to be a member of a group whose symbol was a guy nailed to two pieces of wood.
>
> —George Carlin, comedian

**6.** Acts 4:12 says, "Salvation is found in no one else, for there is no other name under heaven given to men by which we must be saved." What reasons do you think Christianity gives for its assertion that Jesus is the only way to God?

## *Jesus Paid the Price*

The purpose behind the death of Jesus was to make payment for the sins of the world. The Bible makes it clear that the penalty of sin is death. We all have a choice: we can either make that payment ourselves (which falls short and leads to eternal separation from God) or accept the payment Jesus Christ made on our behalf (which pays the price and leads to eternal life with God in his kingdom). Jesus' death on the cross is sufficient to make payment for our sins because he, being God, was without any sin himself. He alone was able to pay the full price. No other religion offers a complete pardon of sin; all others offer either some program for human achievement or a god who overlooks sin and is therefore not holy. In *Know What You Believe,* Paul Little sums it up:

> If Jesus were not fully God, he *could* not be our Savior. But if he were God and yet did nothing on our behalf — that is, did not *do* something to bring us to God — he *would* not be our Savior. Being God *qualified* Jesus Christ to be Savior, but his atoning death for us *made* him our Savior. Jesus not only *could* save men; he *did*.

> If Socrates should enter the room, we would all rise and do him honor. But if Jesus Christ came into the room, we would all fall down and worship him.
>
> —Napoleon

**7.** What is it about Jesus that, according to the Bible, enabled him to become the only worthy payment for sin and therefore the only possible bridge between God and all humankind?

### The Battle of the Wills

Jesus faced the greatest struggle of his life when he decided to give up his life on our behalf.

> The reason my Father loves me is that I lay down my life — only to take it up again. No one takes it from me, but I lay it down of my own accord. I have authority to lay it down and authority to take it up again. This command I received from my Father.
>
> — John 10:17–18

> Jesus went with his disciples to a place called Gethsemane . . . and he began to be sorrowful and troubled. Then he said to them, "My soul is overwhelmed with sorrow to the point of death. Stay here and keep watch with me." Going a little farther, he fell with his face to the ground and prayed, "My Father, if it is possible, may this cup be taken from me. Yet not as I will, but as you will."
>
> — Matthew 26:36–39

## HEART OF THE MATTER

Because of the Resurrection, we know we are not trusting in a myth; we know that our sins are actually forgiven through the death of Christ. Certainty and forgiveness are based on the empty tomb! Christ is the only One who has ever come back from death to tell men about the beyond. In His words we know we have the authoritative Word of God Himself.

—Paul Little,
*Know Why You Believe*

**8.** According to the above verses, what choice did Jesus have in laying down his life for us? How does your answer impact you?

**9.** In what ways can you relate to the struggle Jesus faced in following the will of the Father? Describe a time when you chose to do the right thing even though it was a personal sacrifice for you.

**10.** In what ways is Jesus' life, death, and resurrection an example to you of how to live your life?

**11.** Why is Jesus' resurrection proof of his ability to keep his promises?

**12.** What difference does it make to you personally that Jesus Christ came into the world, lived a perfect life, died on the cross for your sins, and rose again?

## CHARTING YOUR JOURNEY

**13.** Check the statement(s) below that best describes your position at this point. Share your selection with the rest of the group and give reasons for your response.

_____ I don't think Jesus is necessary as a mediator to reach God.

_____ If God really cares and loves me the way the Bible claims he does, I still don't understand why I need a middleman.

_____ This lesson only confirms my fears that God is too big, too high, and too unreachable.

_____ I'm not certain what relevance Jesus has for us today.

_____ I understand that Jesus is the only way to get to God, but I'm not sure how I feel about it.

_____ I have more understanding about Jesus' role in my life than I did before.

_____ I understand that Jesus is the one and only way for me to be reconciled to God.

_____ I understand that the only way to have a relationship with God is through Jesus; however, I am unwilling or not ready to take that step.

_____ I understand the need for Jesus, since he is the only way I can be reconciled to God, and I want to take that step.

_____ Write your own brief phrase here: _____

_____

_____

## Scripture for Further Study

- Matthew 7:21–27
- Matthew 10:32–33
- Matthew 28:1–7
- Luke 24:36–53
- John 14:1–6, 15–21
- John 17:1–5
- Romans 3:21–26
- Romans 5:6–11
- Philippians 2:5–11
- Hebrews 9:22
- 1 Peter 1:18–19

# Can Someone Like Me Really Change?

## Wishful Thinking?

Remember the story of Cinderella? She wants to go to the ball and meet the prince, but she runs into a series of obstacles. Finally, at the last minute, a fairy godmother grants her wish by providing a gown, a fancy hairdo, and a carriage made from a pumpkin. The only requirement is that Cinderella has to leave the ball before the stroke of midnight, because at that time her true identity will be revealed.

Cinderella spends a magical night at the ball with the prince. But just before midnight she flees from the castle and is out of sight just as her gown turns into rags and the carriage goes back to being a pumpkin. Left with the wonderful memory of an enchanted evening, Cinderella returns to her life as the grungy, ragged-clothed keeper of the cinders.

If we ever have occasion to meet someone important for the first time—whether it's our fiancé's parents or the president of the United States—image is a big deal. We may feel the need to improve our appearance, language, or manners. Or we may go so far as to stretch the truth about our work, our net worth, or our upbringing, to look better than we really are.

Surely, it's the same with coming to God. We can't just waltz into the presence of the Creator of the universe dragging our mistakes and history of poor choices. We first need to clean up our past a bit, get rid of a few bad habits, and renew our resolve to do better next time. We have to make ourselves at least appear a little more acceptable; otherwise, how could God tolerate us and our shortcomings?

Even if by some feat of our will we could clean ourselves up for a short time, it's beyond us to maintain a new and improved front over the long haul. The thought that we might forever need to pretend to be someone we aren't overwhelms us. We might fool others for a while, but we can't fool God like that.

Cinderella eventually marries the prince. His love provides her with all she needs in order to become a true princess. But how many times did she worry about how long this was going to last? Would she eventually wake up only to discover that her transformation was merely a fairy tale?

A long-term change, acceptable to God himself, seems too good to be true. We need more than a fairy godmother who can provide us with a temporary, "till the stroke of midnight" fix. Our hearts and souls need a complete overhaul through the spiritual equivalent of Cinderella's marriage to the prince.

> A bad man is worse when he pretends to be a saint.
>
> —Francis Bacon

## OPEN FOR DISCUSSION

**1.** Describe a time when you felt overwhelmed by a project at work or school. Did the pressure drive you to work harder or were you paralyzed by it? How did you cope with the stress?

**2.** What aspect of living the Christian life seems overwhelming or too difficult to you?

**3.** What do you think is behind the obligation people feel to clean up their act before they can become a Christian?

**4.** What sorts of things do you think a person needs to do before becoming a Christian?

## STRAIGHT TALK

### *Instant Promises*

The Bible clearly teaches that salvation is an event. Forgiveness of sin precedes moral reform and is an instantaneous benefit of faith placed in Christ.

> Two other men, both criminals, were also led out with him to be executed. When they came to the place called the Skull, there they crucified him, along with the criminals — one on his right, the other on his left. . . . One of the criminals who hung there hurled insults at him: "Aren't you the Christ? Save yourself and us!" But the other criminal rebuked him. "Don't you fear God," he said, "since you are under the same sentence?

We are punished justly, for we are getting what our deeds deserve. But this man has done nothing wrong." Then he said, "Jesus, remember me when you come into your kingdom." Jesus answered him, "I tell you the truth, today you will be with me in paradise."

—Luke 23:32–33, 39–43

[When Paul and Silas were in prison at Philippi, the jailer of the prison asked,] "Sirs, what must I do to be saved?" They replied, "Believe in the Lord Jesus, and you will be saved."

—Acts 16:30–31

**5.** In the above two cases, salvation was promised before any possible moral reform could be instituted. If salvation is not a matter of self-improvement, on what basis was this promise made? How does this precedent give you hope?

**6.** Have you ever felt defeated by the feeling that the standards of the Christian life are too hard to measure up to? Why or why not?

### No Noticeable Difference?

In an essay entitled "A Pluralist's View," author John Hick, a former evangelical who left evangelicalism to become a pluralist, states that Christianity can't make a noticeable and permanent difference in a person's life. He writes,

> My own global impression . . . is that the virtues and vices seem to be spread more or less evenly among human beings, regardless of whether they are Christians or — to confine ourselves for the moment to the "great world religions" — Jews, Muslims, Hindu, or Buddhists. But is this what we would expect if Christians have a more complete and direct access to God than anyone else and live in a closer relationship to him, being indwelt by the Holy Spirit? Should not the fruit of the Spirit, which according to Paul is "love, joy, peace, patience, kindness, goodness, faithfulness, gentleness, self-control" (Gal. 5:22–23), be more evident in Christian than in non-Christian lives . . . Yet it does not seem to me that in fact Christians are on average noticeably morally superior to Jews, Muslims, Hindus, or Buddhists.

**7.** Do you agree with the above quote by John Hick? Why or why not? Have you ever known of someone who truly lived the Christian life? What do you think enabled him or her to live as a Christian should?

**8.** In what ways is the Christian life impossible to live? In what ways do you think Jesus Christ makes the Christian life possible to live?

## STRAIGHT TALK

### A New Beginning

The Bible teaches that putting one's faith in Jesus for forgiveness of sin means a whole new start in life, with ongoing changes.

> If anyone is in Christ, he is a new creation; the old has gone, the new has come! All this is from God, who reconciled us to himself through Christ.
>
> —2 Corinthians 5:17–18

> If God is for us, who can be against us? He who did not spare his own Son, but gave him up for us all — how will he not also, along with him, graciously give us all things? . . . I am convinced that neither death nor life, neither angels nor demons, neither the present nor the future, nor any powers, neither height nor depth, nor anything else in all creation, will be able to separate us from the love of God that is in Christ Jesus our Lord.
>
> —Romans 8:31–32, 38–39

> . . . being confident of this, that he who began a good work in you will carry it on to completion until the day of Christ Jesus.
>
> —Philippians 1:6

**9.** How and when does the change a person experiences in becoming a Christian start to happen?

**10.** What role does God play in changing people? Would you describe yourself as a person changed by God? Explain.

## HEART OF THE MATTER

**11.** Would it be intimidating or frightening to you to be known as a committed Christian? Why or why not?

**12.** Do you ever feel that you cannot change enough to live as a Christian? Explain.

**13.** According to the verses in the previous Straight Talk, to what extent does God commit himself to you and to the changes that occur in you? How does this make you feel?

**14.** On a scale from one to ten, place an X near the spot and phrase that best describes you. Share your selection with the rest of the group and give reasons for placing your X where you did.

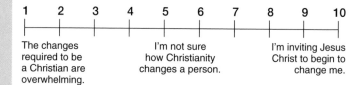

| 1 | 2 | 3 | 4 | 5 | 6 | 7 | 8 | 9 | 10 |

The changes required to be a Christian are overwhelming.

I'm not sure how Christianity changes a person.

I'm inviting Jesus Christ to begin to change me.

## *Scripture for Further Study*

- Deuteronomy 6:5
- Psalm 51:15–17
- Psalm 119:10
- John 15:1–17
- Romans 5:11
- 2 Corinthians 5:7, 17
- Galatians 5:16–26
- Hebrews 11:6
- James 1:22–25
- 1 Peter 5:6–7
- 1 John 1:9

# How Does Someone Actually Become a Christian?

## *Too Good to Be True?*

David sat on the front porch with the latest copy of *Newsweek* facedown across his knee. Normally, he'd be poring over the articles while relaxing in the shade, but today he just couldn't concentrate. It had been two weeks since his last job interview and he still hadn't heard anything. He stared at the crabapple tree, his eyes glazed over. He didn't notice that Anne had joined him on the porch until she touched the cold glass of iced tea against his neck.

"Whoa!" he exclaimed with a jump.

"Here," Anne said, handing him the glass. "You look like you need something refreshing."

"Oh. Thanks," he muttered. He slowly poked the wedge of lemon down to the bottom with the long spoon.

"I just got off the phone with Kim."

David took a sip from his tea. Anne wasn't sure if he was listening, but she continued. "The move is done. They're all settled in their new home. They really like being back in the area."

"Hmm," he grunted. He stared at the misshapen trunk of the tree. He'd planted it himself years ago.

Anne stirred the spoon in her own glass, the sugar at the bottom clouding the tea for a moment. "I don't know if I did the right thing, but I talked to her about your situation. Actually, we first discussed it last month when she was still in Phoenix."

Now he was looking past the tree. "You know, if only I'd staked it better, it wouldn't have grown so crooked."

"David, are you listening to me?" Anne asked.

David set his glass on the porch and sighed. "I need to find a job! It's been eight weeks and I've got nothing. No leads, no more interviews lined up. Anne, we could be sunk. We're depleting our savings."

"But listen to what I'm trying to tell you . . . about what Kim promised."

David stood and started pacing. "I'm beginning to think I made the biggest mistake of my life. I thought a man with my qualifications could step right into something bigger and better. But this job search has been such a long, complicated process. It's just too hard. Look at me! I'm stuck here with no future."

Anne laughed and shook her head. "You're not paying any attention to what I'm saying!" Even her laugh didn't faze him.

"I think I'm going to have to swallow my pride and ask Bill for my crummy old job back."

Anne leaned in close, face-to-face with David. "Listen to me! Kim is a very important player now at Grayson Technology. When I told her you were hoping for something there, she made a few calls. With your qualifications and a good word from her, you're as good as in. David, that job is a perfect fit and all you have to do is accept it!"

David laughed sarcastically. "Yeah, right!"

"What?" Anne demanded.

"Nothing's that easy. I'm sure there's a catch of some kind."

"No, David. Don't you get it? Kim is the head of Human Resources now! She's already put in a good

What must we do to do the works God requires?

—a man in a crowd listening to Jesus (John 6:28)

What must I do to be saved?

—the man in charge of the jail at Philippi, to his prisoners Paul and Silas (Acts 16:30)

word for you, and there's nothing else for you to do but say yes! All you have to do is accept the position and it's yours."

"I'd love to believe it's that simple. I'm sure there's more to it than that. But after all I've been through . . ." David fought back the desire to give in to the hope that was dawning in him.

Anne reached for his hands and whispered, "That job is everything you've been looking and hoping for." She smiled. "Don't let it slip away just because it seems too good to be true. It's yours for the asking."

> There is one God and one mediator between God and men, the man Jesus Christ.
> —1 Timothy 2:5

## OPEN FOR DISCUSSION

1. When you first heard about Christianity, what did you think was its message? How would you summarize that message now, to the best of your understanding?

2. Do you think becoming a Christian is an ongoing process, something that happens at a specific point in time, or a combination of the two? Give reasons for your answer.

**3.** If salvation is a free gift, isn't it automatically applied to everyone—even atheists? Why or why not?

## STRAIGHT TALK

### *Exchanging Vows*

Two people meet, spend time together, and start to really get to know one another. They discover how much they have in common and uncover each other's likes and dislikes, along with a few idiosyncrasies. But though they may know each other very well — even love each other deeply — that still doesn't make them married.

What is it that makes a couple married? The gift of marriage is given and received on the basis of a promise. Any couple who want to be married must face that once-and-for-all act in which they exchange vows to seal their commitment. The man and woman say, "I do" — "I want to be united to you" — and they accept each other as a spouse. From that point forward they live as a married couple.

In a similar way, a person may hear about God and get to know all about him over time. The person may know a lot about Christianity and the Bible, and may even attend church services and know a few Christians personally, but that does not mean the person is a Christian. He or she may even grow to love God and everything that Christianity represents, but that still doesn't make the person a Christian. What is it that makes a person a Christian? It may come about through a gradual process, but a person must face that once-and-for-all act in which he or she is sealed in the Holy Spirit through exchanging a vow. The person says, "I do" — "I want to be forgiven and be united to God." The person accepts Jesus as forgiver and leader of his or her life. At that point the gift of salvation is given and received and the person moves forward to living life as a Christian.

**4.** Do you agree or disagree with the previous analogy? Explain. What stage are you in right now: the "getting to know you" stage, the "ready to make a commitment" stage, or the "I've already said 'I do'" stage? Why do you think becoming a Christian requires an intentional response?

**5.** What is the difference between an intellectual assent to a set of beliefs and an actual acceptance of those same beliefs?

## STRAIGHT TALK

### *Jump in the Wheelbarrow*

To intellectually assent to Christianity would be to acknowledge, as a piece of information, that Jesus came into the world to save sinners. Acceptance is receiving that benefit for yourself. Years ago the Great Karl Wallenda, an acrobat, stretched a wire across Niagara Falls and offered to carry anyone across in a wheelbarrow. There were many who "believed" he could do it, but no takers. To actually get in the wheelbarrow and be taken across the chasm — that's the difference between intellectual assent and acceptance.

**6.** If you must do something to be worthy of salvation, it can't be a gift. Yet the Bible says, "To all who received him, to those who believed [trusted] in his name, he gave the right to become children of God" (John 1:12). What does it mean to "receive" Jesus? How is *receiving* a gift different from *earning* it?

**7.** In John 5:24 Jesus says, "I tell you the truth, whoever hears my word and believes him who sent me has eternal life and will not be condemned; he has crossed over from death to life." And John 1:12 says, "To all who received him, to those who believed in his name, he gave the right to become children of God." According to these verses, what do we need to do to receive eternal life? What does God do?

Being a Christian is not just a good way to die, it's the best way to live.

—Bill Hybels, senior pastor, Willow Creek Community Church

**8.** Some people think of salvation as preparing for a quiz. They think the important thing is to learn the right answer to the question, asked by God, "Why should I let you into heaven?" Why do you think this misses the point of what God wants from a relationship with us?

**9.** Jesus described the essence of eternal life when he said, "This is eternal life: that they may know you, the only true God, and Jesus Christ, whom you have sent" (John 17:3). The phrase "to know" can also mean "to share intimately." What light does this shed on the true meaning of eternal life and on God's intention for our relationship with him?

> Thou has made us for Thyself, O Lord, and our hearts are restless till they rest in Thee.
>
> —Saint Augustine

## STRAIGHT TALK

### *Take the Test*

The Bible warns that it is so important to carefully consider where you are in your spiritual journey and to be intentional about making a response. The natural tendency is to trivialize these matters, when in fact they ought to be taken seriously. Your eternal destiny weighs in the balance.

> Examine yourselves to see whether you are in the faith; test yourselves. Do you not realize that Christ Jesus is in you — unless, of course, you fail the test?
>
> — 2 Corinthians 13:5

> My dear friends . . . continue to work out your salvation with fear and trembling.
>
> — Philippians 2:12

> If we claim to be without sin, we deceive ourselves and the truth is not in us. If we confess our sins, he is faithful and just and will forgive us our sins and purify us from all unrighteousness.
>
> — 1 John 1:8–9

This is the testimony: God has given us eternal life, and this life is in his Son. He who has the Son has life; he who does not have the Son of God does not have life.

— 1 John 5:11–12

Enter through the narrow gate. For wide is the gate and broad is the road that leads to destruction, and many enter through it. But small is the gate and narrow the road that leads to life, and only a few find it.

— Matthew 7:13–14

## HEART OF THE MATTER

**10.** Draw a line. On one side put yourself, on the other put God. Does any obstacle prevent you from crossing that line, once and for all, and embracing God's forgiveness and leadership? Explain your answer.

**11.** Romans 10:9 says, "If you confess with your mouth, 'Jesus is Lord,' and believe in your heart that God raised him from the dead, you will be saved." Does anything keep you from declaring the resurrected Jesus as the forgiver and leader of your life? If you're comfortable doing so, tell the group where you are with this decision. If there is anything holding you back, share that as well.

# STRAIGHT TALK

## *It's Party Time!*

If at some point in this series, or even during this session, you have settled this matter of where you stand with God and have received Jesus as your Savior, then it's party time to celebrate! Jesus says to all who know him, "'Rejoice with me; I have found my lost sheep.' I tell you that in the same way there will be . . . rejoicing in heaven over one sinner who repents" (Luke 15:6–7). If you still have questions or need time to process this information, do whatever it takes to get this matter settled.

> No one can sum up all God is able to accomplish through one solitary life, wholly yielded, adjusted and obedient to him.
>
> —D. L. Moody

**12.** What's your reaction to the word of encouragement offered in the Straight Talk above? What, to you, would feel like the right thing to do at this point in this series of studies? Where would you like to go from here?

**13.** If you could ask God one question you knew he would answer right away, what would it be?

As for you, you were dead in your transgressions and sins, in which you used to live when you followed the ways of this world. . . . But because of his great love for us, God, who is rich in mercy, made us alive with Christ even when we were dead in transgressions—it is by grace you have been saved. And God raised us up with Christ and seated us with him in the heavenly realms in Christ Jesus, in order that in the coming ages he might show the incomparable riches of his grace, expressed in his kindness to us in Christ Jesus. For it is by grace you have been saved, through faith—and this is not from yourselves, it is the gift of God—not by works, so that no one can boast. For we are God's workmanship, created in Christ Jesus to do good works, which God prepared in advance for us to do.

—Ephesians 2:1–2, 4–10

**14.** On a scale from one to ten, place an X near the spot and phrase that best describes you. Share your selection with the rest of the group and give reasons for placing your X where you did.

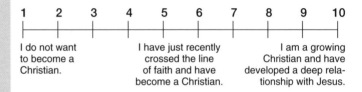

1 — I do not want to become a Christian.

5 — I have just recently crossed the line of faith and have become a Christian.

10 — I am a growing Christian and have developed a deep relationship with Jesus.

## Scripture for Further Study

- Psalm 51:10
- Proverbs 3:5–6
- Matthew 7:24–29
- Matthew 6:24–28
- Mark 8:34–38
- Luke 9:57–62
- Luke 19:1–10

- John 5:24
- Romans 10:10
- 2 Corinthians 6:2
- Ephesians 2:8–9
- 1 Peter 1:1–9
- Revelation 3:20

# Recommended Resources

Ken Boa and Larry Moody, *I'm Glad You Asked* (Chariot Victor, 1995).

Gregory Boyd and Edward Boyd, *Letters from a Skeptic* (Chariot Victor, 1994).

Billy Graham, *How to Be Born Again* (Word, 1989).

David Hewetson and David Miller, *Christianity Made Simple* (InterVarsity, 1983).

Cliffe Knechtle, *Give Me an Answer* (InterVarsity, 1986).

Cliffe Knechtle, *Help Me Believe* (InterVarsity, 2000).

Peter Kreeft and Ronald Tacelli, *Handbook of Christian Apologetics* (InterVarsity, 1994).

Robert A. Laidlaw, *The Reason Why* (Bridge-Logos, 1994).

C. S. Lewis, *Mere Christianity* (HarperSanFransisco, 2001).

Paul Little, *Know What You Believe* (Chariot Victor, 1987).

Paul Little, *Know Why You Believe* (InterVarsity, 2000).

Max Lucado, *He Did This Just for You* (Nelson, 2001).

Walter Martin, *Kingdom of the Cults* (Bethany, 1997).

Fritz Ridenour, *So What's the Difference?* (Regal, 2001).

John R. W. Stott, *Basic Christianity* (Eerdmans, 1986).

Lee Strobel, *The Case for Christ* (Zondervan, 1998).

Lee Strobel, *The Case for Faith* (Zondervan, 2000).

**WILLOW CREEK ASSOCIATION®**

**WILLOW CREEK RESOURCES**

# Willow Creek Association
*Vision, Training, Resources for Prevailing Churches*

This resource was created to serve you and to help you in building a local church that prevails!

Since 1992, the Willow Creek Association (WCA) has been linking like-minded, action-oriented churches with each other and with strategic vision, training, and resources. Now a worldwide network of over 6,400 churches from more than ninety denominations, the WCA works to equip Member Churches and others with the tools needed to build prevailing churches. Our desire is to inspire, equip, and encourage Christian leaders to build biblically functioning churches that reach increasing numbers of unchurched people, not just with innovations from Willow Creek Community Church in South Barrington, Illinois, but from any church in the world that has experienced God-given breakthroughs.

### WILLOW CREEK CONFERENCES

Each year, thousands of local church leaders, staff and volunteers—from WCA Member Churches and others—attend one of our conferences or training events. Conferences offered on the Willow Creek campus in South Barrington, Illinois, include:

**Prevailing Church Conference:** Foundational training for staff and volunteers working to build a prevailing local church.

**Prevailing Church Workshops:** More than fifty strategic, day-long workshops covering seven topic areas that represent key characteristics of a prevailing church; offered twice each year.

**Promiseland Conference:** Children's ministries; infant through fifth grade.

**Student Ministries Conference:** Junior and senior high ministries.

**Willow Creek Arts Conference:** Vision and training for Christian artists using their gifts in the ministries of local churches.

**Leadership Summit:** Envisioning and equipping Christians with leadership gifts and responsibilities; broadcast live via satellite to eighteen cities across North America.

**Contagious Evangelism Conference:** Encouragement and training for churches and church leaders who want to be strategic in reaching lost people for Christ.

**Small Groups Conference:** Exploring how developing a church *of* small groups can play a vital role in developing authentic Christian community that leads to spiritual transformation.

To find out more about WCA conferences, visit our website at www.willowcreek.com.

### PREVAILING CHURCH REGIONAL WORKSHOPS

Each year the WCA team leads several, two-day training events in select cities across the United States. Some twenty day-long workshops are offered in topic areas including leadership, next-generation ministries, small groups, arts and worship, evangelism, spiritual gifts, financial stewardship, and spiritual formation. These events make quality training more accessible and affordable to larger groups of staff and volunteers.

To find out more about Prevailing Church Regional Workshops, visit our website at www.willowcreek.com.

## WILLOW CREEK RESOURCES™

Churches can look to Willow Creek Resources™ for a trusted channel of ministry tools in areas of leadership, evangelism, spiritual gifts, small groups, drama, contemporary music, financial stewardship, spiritual transformation, and more. For ordering information, call (800) 570-9812 or visit our website at www.willowcreek.com.

## WCA MEMBERSHIP

Membership in the Willow Creek Association as well as attendance at WCA Conferences is for churches, ministries, and leaders who hold to a historic, orthodox understanding of biblical Christianity. The annual church membership fee of $249 provides substantial discounts for your entire team on all conferences and Willow Creek Resources, networking opportunities with other outreach-oriented churches, a bimonthly newsletter, a subscription to the *Defining Moments* monthly audio journal for leaders, and more.

To find out more about WCA membership, visit our website at www.willowcreek.com.

## WILLOWNET (WWW.WILLOWCREEK.COM)

This Internet resource service provides access to hundreds of Willow Creek messages, drama scripts, songs, videos, and multimedia ideas. The system allows you to sort through these elements and download them for a fee.

Our website also provides detailed information on the Willow Creek Association, Willow Creek Community Church, WCA membership, conferences, training events, resources, and more.

## WILLOWCHARTS.COM (WWW.WILLOWCHARTS.COM)

Designed for local church worship leaders and musicians, WillowCharts.com provides online access to hundreds of music charts and chart components, including choir, orchestral, and horn sections, as well as rehearsal tracks and video streaming of Willow Creek Community Church performances.

## THE NET (HTTP://STUDENTMINISTRY.WILLOWCREEK.COM)

The NET is an online training and resource center designed by and for student ministry leaders. It provides an inside look at the structure, vision, and mission of prevailing student ministries from around the world. The NET gives leaders access to complete programming elements, including message outlines, dramas, small group questions, and more. An indispensable resource and networking tool for prevailing student ministry leaders!

## CONTACT THE WILLOW CREEK ASSOCIATION

If you have comments or questions, or would like to find out more about WCA events or resources, please contact us:

### Willow Creek Association
P.O. Box 3188, Barrington, IL 60011-3188
Phone: (800) 570-9812 or (847) 765-0070
Fax: (888) 922-0035 or (847) 765-5046
Web: www.willowcreek.com

# TOUGH QUESTIONS

## Garry Poole and Judson Poling

"The profound insights and candor captured in these guides will sharpen your mind, soften your heart, and inspire you and the members of your group to find vital answers together."                    —Bill Hybels

This second edition of Tough Questions, designed for use in any small group setting, is ideal for use in seeker small groups. Based on more than five years of field-tested feedback, extensive revisions make this best-selling series easier to use and more appealing than ever for both participants and group leaders.

Softcover

| | |
|---|---|
| *How Does Anyone Know God Exists?* | ISBN 0-310-24502-8 |
| *What Difference Does Jesus Make?* | ISBN 0-310-24503-6 |
| *How Reliable Is the Bible?* | ISBN 0-310-24504-4 |
| *How Could God Allow Suffering and Evil?* | ISBN 0-310-24505-2 |
| *Don't All Religions Lead to God?* | ISBN 0-310-24506-0 |
| *Do Science and the Bible Conflict?* | ISBN 0-310-24507-9 |
| *Why Become a Christian?* | ISBN 0-310-24508-7 |
| *Leader's Guide* | ISBN 0-310-24509-5 |

*Pick up a copy at your favorite local bookstore today!*

GRAND RAPIDS, MICHIGAN 49530 USA

WWW.ZONDERVAN.COM

# THE THREE HABITS OF HIGHLY CONTAGIOUS CHRISTIANS

### Garry Poole

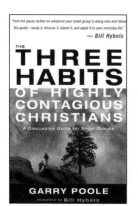

**A small group discussion guide that will ignite the heart to reach seekers for Christ.**

Living an intentionally contagious Christian life really matters! It's worth the effort and risks involved. *The Three Habits of Highly Contagious Christians* will help you reach out to seekers naturally by

1. building relationships
2. sharing a verbal witness
3. inviting people to outreach events

Discover how to cultivate authentic relationships with seekers, not as projects to work on but as friends and companions with common interests. You'll learn practical ways to build bridges of trust while checking yourself for the underlying attitudes that drive seekers away. From being on the lookout for windows of opportunity to talk with seekers about Christ, to bringing them to a church service or outreach, this study helps you find ways to bring people to Christ easily and naturally.

Each session begins with a thought-provoking story, then uses questions that generate honest, open group discussion. Exercises encourage participants to apply principles to their own lives. *The Three Habits of Highly Contagious Christians* challenges believers to individually commit to specific choices that could make all the difference in the lives of seeking friends and family members.

Softcover: ISBN 0-310-24496-X

*Pick up a copy at your favorite local bookstore today!*

WILLOW CREEK
RESOURCES

ZONDERVAN™

GRAND RAPIDS, MICHIGAN 49530 USA
WWW.ZONDERVAN.COM

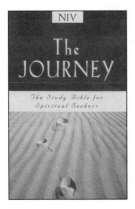

# REALITY CHECK SERIES

## by Mark Ashton

### Winning at Life

Learn the secrets Jesus taught his disciples about winning at life through the stories he told.

### Jesus' Greatest Moments

Uncover the facts and meaning of the provocative events of the final week of Jesus.

### Leadership Jesus Style

Learn the leadership principles taught and lived by Jesus.

### Hot Issues

Find out how Jesus addressed the challenges of racism, feminism, sexuality, materialism, poverty, and intolerance.

### When Tragedy Strikes

Discover Jesus' perspective on the problem of suffering and evil in the world.

### Future Shock

Uncover Jesus' perspective on the mysteries of the future as revealed in the Bible.

### Sudden Impact

Discover the life-changing power of Jesus as he interacted with his contemporaries.

### Clear Evidence

Weigh the arguments for and against the Jesus of the Bible.

| | |
|---|---|
| Winning at Life | ISBN 0-310-24525-7 |
| Jesus' Greatest Moments | ISBN 0-310-24528-1 |
| Leadership Jesus Style | ISBN 0-310-24526-5 |
| Hot Issues | ISBN 0-310-24523-0 |
| When Tragedy Strikes | ISBN 0-310-24524-9 |
| Future Shock | ISBN 0-310-24527-3 |
| Sudden Impact | ISBN 0-310-24522-2 |
| Clear Evidence | ISBN 0-310-24746-2 |

*Pick up a copy at your favorite local bookstore today!*

# THE CASE FOR FAITH

## Lee Strobel

**Was God telling the truth when he said, "You will seek me and find me when you seek me with all your heart"?**

In his best-seller *The Case for Christ*, the legally trained investigative reporter Lee Strobel examined the claims of Christ, reaching the hard-won yet satisfying verdict that Jesus is God's unique Son.

But despite the compelling historical evidence that Strobel presented, many grapple with doubts or serious concerns about faith in God. As in a court of law, they want to shout, "Objection!" They say, "If God is love, then what about all of the suffering that festers in our world?" Or, 'If Jesus is the door to heaven, then what about the millions who have never heard of him?"

In *The Case for Faith*, Strobel turns his tenacious investigative skills to the most persistent emotional objections to belief, the eight "heart" barriers to faith. *The Case for Faith* is for those who may be feeling attracted to Jesus but who are faced with formidable intellectual barriers standing squarely in their path. For Christians, it will deepen their convictions and give them fresh confidence in discussing Christianity with even their most skeptical friends.

| | |
|---|---|
| Hardcover | ISBN 0-310-22015-7 |
| Softcover | ISBN 0-310-23469-7 |
| Evangelism Pack | ISBN 0-310-23508-1 |
| Mass Market-6 pack | ISBN 0-310-23509-X |
| Abridged Audio Pages® Cassette | ISBN 0-310-23475-1 |
| Unabridged Audio Pages® Cassette | ISBN 0-310-24825-6 |
| Unabridged Audio Pages® CD | ISBN 0-310-24787-X |
| Student Edition | ISBN 0-310-24188-X |
| Student Edition 6-Pack (with Leader's Guide) | ISBN 0-310-24922-8 |

# THE CASE FOR CHRIST

### Lee Strobel

Is Jesus really the divine Son of God? What reason is there to believe that he is?

In this best-seller, investigative reporter Lee Strobel examines the claims of Christ. Written in the style of a blockbuster investigative report, *The Case for Christ* puts the toughest questions about Christ to experts in the fields of science, psychology, law, medicine, biblical studies, and more.

The result is a powerful narrative that will convince seekers and believers alike of the proven reality of Jesus Christ.

"Lee Strobel asks the questions a tough-minded skeptic would ask. Every inquirer should have it."

—Phillip E. Johnson, law professor,
University of California at Berkeley

| | |
|---|---|
| Hardcover | ISBN 0-310-22646-5 |
| Softcover | ISBN 0-310-20930-7 |
| Evangelism Pack | ISBN 0-310-22605-8 |
| Mass Market 6-pack | ISBN 0-310-22627-9 |
| Abridged Audio Pages® Cassette | ISBN 0-310-21960-4 |
| Unabridged Audio Pages® Cassette | ISBN 0-310-24825-6 |
| Unabridged Audio Pages® CD | ISBN 0-310-24779-9 |
| Student Edition | ISBN 0-310-23484-0 |
| Student Edition 6-Pack with Leader's Guide | ISBN 0-310-24851-5 |

*Pick up a copy at your favorite local bookstore today!*

GRAND RAPIDS, MICHIGAN 49530 USA

WWW.ZONDERVAN.COM